SEASONS
Spring

Kay Barnham

WAYLAND

Explore the world with **Popcorn** - your complete first non-fiction library.

Look out for more titles in the **Popcorn** range. All books have the same format of simple text and awesome images. Text is carefully matched to the pictures to help readers to identify and understand key vocabulary.
www.waylandbooks.co.uk/popcorn

First published in 2009 by Wayland

Wayland
Hachette Children's Books
338 Euston Road
London NW1 3BH

Wayland Australia
Level 17/207 Kent Street
Sydney NSW 2000

Senior Editor: Claire Shanahan
Designer: Ruth Cowan
Picture Researcher: Louise Edgeworth
Concept Designer: Paul Cherrill

British Library Cataloguing in Publication Data:
Barnham, Kay
Spring. - (Popcorn. Seasons ; v. 2)
1. Spring - Juvenile literature
I. Title
508.2

ISN: 978 07502 5787 9

Printed and bound in China

Wayland is a division of Hachette Children's Books,
an Hachette UK Company.
www.hachettelivre.co.uk

Acknowledgements:
Alamy: Arco Images GmbH Imprint page, David Noton Photography p4-5, Dennis Hallinan p7, Redmond Durrell p10, Nigel Cattlin p14, Arco Images GmbH p15, Foodfolio p17, Joe Fox p19; Corbis: Paul Barton p6, Yujiro Matsuo/amanaimages p8, Julia Thorne/Robert Harding World Imagery p12; Getty: American Images Inc Title page, David Seed Photography p9, Superstudio p16, American Images Inc p18; Dreamstime: © Gemphotography p11, COVER; IStockphoto: p13.

Contents

The seasons

There are four seasons in the year.
The seasons are called spring, summer,
autumn and winter. Each season is different.

In spring, the days become warmer and longer. The spring months are March, April and May.

Spring weather

The weather gets warmer in spring. May is often one of the sunniest months of the year.

Early mornings can still be chilly.

At this time of year, the weather can change a lot. There may be rain, sun, wind or snow – all on the same day!

Sudden showers are common.

Spring trees

Spring is a time of new life. Plants, trees and grass start to grow. Fruit trees, like cherry trees and plum trees, grow blossom.

The wind blows blossom from the trees. Brand new leaves are left behind.

Seeds that fell from trees
in autumn begin to sprout.
Soon, they will grow into
tiny plants called saplings.

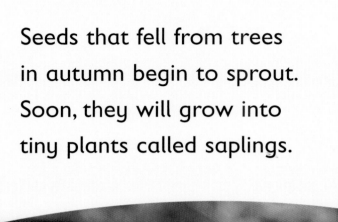

This is an oak
sapling. Oak trees
may live up to a
thousand years!

Spring flowers

In spring, lots of flowers appear.
First, shoots push up through the
soil. Then the stems grow tall.

Buds open to show
the beautiful petals
inside.

petals

bud

stem

Bluebells flower in April and May. They grow in woods and forests.

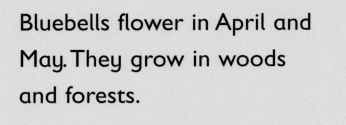

In the UK, bluebells are protected by law because they are so rare.

11

Spring animals

Spring is the time of year when lambs are born. A lamb drinks milk from its mother. When it is older, it will eat grass.

A ewe is pregnant for about five months before giving birth to lambs.

Baby birds hatch from eggs.
The mother brings her chicks food
to eat. When the chicks grows bigger,
they will find their own food.

Birds' nests can be made of twigs, grass and leaves.

Fun in spring

Spring is an exciting time to explore the countryside. Look out for frogspawn in ponds or streams. Frogspawn is a mass of frog's eggs.

Each black dot takes three or four months to turn into a frog.

14

Spring is a good time to visit a farm. There, you will see many baby animals, such as piglets, calves, ducklings and chicks.

How many ducklings can you see?

Spring food

Spring is the best time to plant vegetables such as carrots, peas and potatoes.

Seeds and seedlings must be watered often, so they grow.

16

At this time of year, rhubarb is ripe and ready to eat.

Rhubarb can be made into delicious puddings like this rhubarb crumble.

17

Spring festivals

In the UK and USA, spring happens near the beginning of the year. The festivals of Easter and Passover are both celebrated in spring.

Have you ever taken part in an Easter-egg hunt?

On 17 March, Irish people around
the world celebrate St Patrick's Day.
St Patrick is the patron saint of Ireland.

These people
are taking part
in a St Patrick's
Day parade.

Why do we have seasons?

We have seasons because Earth is tilted. As Earth moves around the Sun, different parts of the planet are nearer the Sun.

In **spring**, our part of the planet moves towards the Sun. The weather grows warmer.

In **summer**, our part of the planet is nearest the Sun. This means that the weather is hot.

In **autumn**, our part of the planet moves away from the Sun. The weather grows cooler.

In **winter**, our part of the planet is furthest from the Sun. This means that the weather is cold.

It takes a year for the four seasons
to happen. This is because it takes
a year for Earth to move around the Sun.

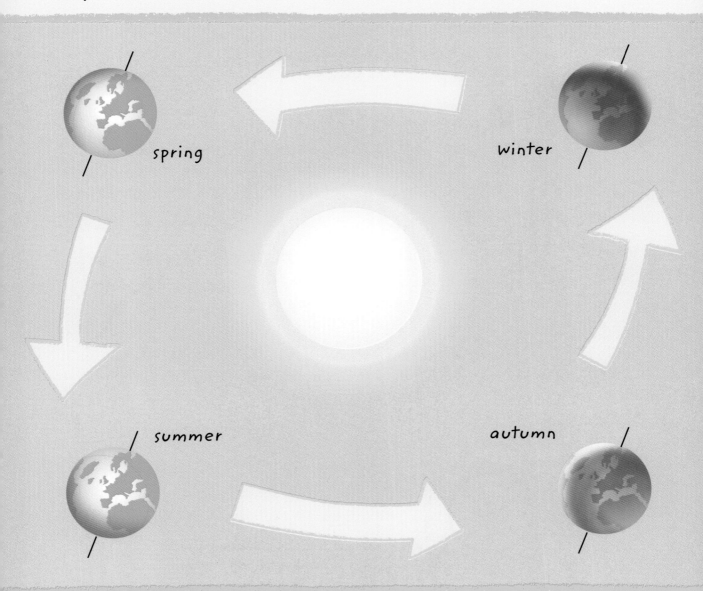

spring

winter

summer

autumn

Make a weather chart

Keep a record of the weather in spring.

1. Draw a calendar for each month of spring, with a box for each day.

2. On each day, record whether it has been sunny, cloudy, rainy or snowy. Use a symbol for each kind of weather.

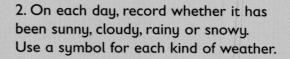

3. If it has been sunny, write down how many hours of sun there were.

4. Leave a measuring jug outside. If it has been raining, check the measuring jug to see how many centimetres of rain have fallen.

5. Each day, check your thermometer and write down how warm or cold it has been.

6. At the end of each month, look back at your chart. You might be surprised at how many different types of weather there have been!

Glossary

blossom the flowers on a tree

ewe a female sheep

patron a saint who is thought of as protecting a place or activity

petal one of the coloured parts of a flower

pregnant when an animal or human is expecting a baby

sapling a young tree

seedling a young plant, often grown from a seed

shoot a new part of a plant

sprout to begin to grow

stem the main part of a plant, which grows above the ground

Index

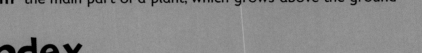